# Garfield

## We Love You Too

JIM

RAVETTE BOOKS

First published by Ravette Books Limited 1985
Reprinted 1986, 1987
This edition first published 1988

Printed and bound in Great Britain
for Ravette Books Limited,
3 Glenside Estate, Star Road, Partridge Green,
Horsham, Sussex RH13 8RA
by Cox & Wyman Ltd, Reading

ISBN 0 906710 75 8

© 1981 United Feature Syndicate, Inc.

5-12

© 1981 United Feature Syndicate, Inc.

GUESS WHAT, GARFIELD? WE ARE GOING BACK TO THE FARM

9-21

JIM DAVIS

IT WILL BE NICE TO GET BACK IN TOUCH WITH MOTHER NATURE

WHEN YOU FIND HER, GIVE HER MY BEST

CLICK

ARRGH!

JIM DAVIS

SORRY, GARFIELD

I WISH YOU'D WARN ME

10-24

HA HA. HOW CAN I RESIST YOU WHEN YOU'RE CUTE? HELP YOURSELF, GARFIELD

JIM DAVIS

A FOOL AND HIS LASAGNA ARE SOON PARTED

© 1981 United Feature Syndicate, Inc.

© 1981 United Feature Syndicate, Inc.

BAP!

6-10    JIM DAVIS

WOINNG

WOINNG

© 1981 United Feature Syndicate, Inc.

© 1981 United Feature Syndicate, Inc

© 1981 United Feature Syndicate, Inc.

© 1981 United Feature Syndicate, Inc.

© 1984 United Feature Syndicate, Inc.

© 1984 United Feature Syndicate, Inc.  12-28

© 1984 United Feature Syndicate, Inc.

© 1984 United Feature Syndicate, Inc.

© JIM DAVIS 9-10

WHY, THANK YOU, GARFIELD!

PSHHH

© 1984 United Feature Syndicate, Inc.

JIM DAVIS    9-28

© 1984 United Feature Syndicate, Inc.

© 1984 United Feature Syndicate, Inc.

© 1984 United Feature Syndicate, Inc.

© 1984 United Feature Syndicate, Inc.

© 1984 United Feature Syndicate, Inc.

© 1964 United Feature Syndicate, Inc.

© 1984 United Feature Syndicate, Inc.

© 1984 United Feature Syndicate, Inc.

© 1984 United Feature Syndicate, Inc.

LET'S SEE HOW I DID ON MY DIET THIS WEEK

WHIMPER

OH, SHUT UP

© 1984 United Feature Syndicate inc. JIM DAVIS

10-18

© 1984 United Feature Syndicate, Inc.

© 1984 United Feature Syndicate, Inc.

© 1984 United Feature Syndicate, Inc.

© 1984 United Feature Syndicate, Inc.

1-12-85

SLUP!

© 1985 United Feature Syndicate, Inc.

THAT WAS MY LAST CUP OF COFFEE!

I SPILLED SOME. YOU CAN SUCK IT OUT OF MY SWEATER

1-14

© 1985 United Feature Syndicate, Inc.

© 1985 United Feature Syndicate,inc.

## OTHER GARFIELD BOOKS IN THIS SERIES

## LANDSCAPE SERIES

## COLOUR TV SPECIALS

| | |
|---|---|
| Here Comes Garfield | £2.95 |
| Garfield On The Town | £2.95 |
| Garfield In The Rough | £2.95 |
| Garfield In Disguise | £2.95 |
| Garfield In Paradise | £2.95 |
| Garfield Goes To Hollywood | £2.95 |
| A Garfield Christmas | £2.95 |

## COLOUR TREASURIES

| | |
|---|---|
| The Second Garfield Treasury | £5.95 |
| The Third Garfield Treasury | £5.95 |
| The Fourth Garfield Treasury | £5.95 |
| | |
| Garfield A Weekend Away | £4.95 |

All these books are available at your local bookshop or newsagent, or can be ordered direct from the publisher. Just tick the titles you require and fill in the form below. Prices and availability subject to change without notice.

Ravette Books Limited, 3 Glenside Estate, Star Road, Partridge Green, Horsham, West Sussex RH13 8RA

Please send a cheque or postal order, and allow the following for postage and packing. UK: Pocket-books and TV Specials – 45p for one book plus 20p for the second book and 15p for each additional book. Landscape Series – 45p for one book plus 30p for each additional book. Treasuries and A Weekend Away – 85p for one book plus 60p for each additional book.

Name ............................................................................................

Address .......................................................................................

............................................................................................